Copyright © 1985 by John Burningham
All rights reserved. No part of this book may be reproduced
or transmitted in any form or by any means, electronic or mechanical,
including photocopying, recording, or by any information storage
and retrieval system, without permission in writing from the publisher.
Originally published in Great Britain by
Walker Books, Ltd., 184–192 Drummond Street, London NW1 3HP
Published in the United States in 1986 by Crown Publishers, Inc.,
225 Park Avenue South, New York, New York 10003
CROWN is a trademark of Crown Publishers, Inc.
IT'S GREAT TO LEARN! and logo
are trademarks of Crown Publishers, Inc.
Manufactured in Italy

Library of Congress Cataloging in Publication Data
Burningham, John. John Burningham's Colors.
Summary: Pictures of purple grapes, white snow,
green frogs, and other objects introduce eleven
common colors.
1. Color—Juvenile literature. [1. Color]
I. Title. II. Title: Colors.
QC495.5.B87 1986 535.6 85-12582
ISBN 0-517-55961-7
10 9 8 7 6 5 4 3 2 1
First American Edition

John Burningham's

Colors

CROWN PUBLISHERS, INC.   NEW YORK

red

yellow

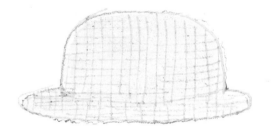

blue

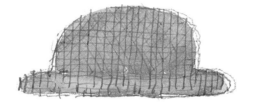

gray

purple

white

orange

green

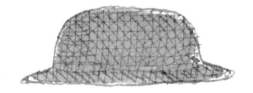

brown

pink

black

red
yellow
blue
gray
purple
white
orange
green
brown
pink
black